Moments Together

for

GROWING CLOSER TO GOD

DENNIS *and* BARBARA RAINEY

Regal

From Gospel Light
Ventura, California, U.S.A.

Regal

PUBLISHED BY REGAL BOOKS
FROM GOSPEL LIGHT
VENTURA, CALIFORNIA, U.S.A.
PRINTED IN THE U.S.A.

Regal Books is a ministry of Gospel Light, an evangelical Christian publisher dedicated to serving the local church. We believe God's vision for Gospel Light is to provide church leaders with biblical, user-friendly materials that will help them evangelize, disciple and minister to children, youth and families.

It is our prayer that this Regal book will help you discover biblical truth for your own life and help you meet the needs of others. May God richly bless you.

For a free catalog of resources from Regal Books/Gospel Light, please call your Christian supplier or contact us at 1-800-4-GOSPEL or www.regalbooks.com.

Rights for publishing this book in other languages are contracted by Gospel Light Worldwide, the international non-profit ministry of Gospel Light. Gospel Light Worldwide also provides publishing and technical assistance to international publishers dedicated to producing Sunday School and Vacation Bible School curricula and books in the languages of the world. For additional information, visit www.gospellightworldwide.org; write to Gospel Light Worldwide, P.O. Box 3875, Ventura, CA 93006; or send an e-mail to info@gospellightworldwide.org.

The publisher regrets the omission of credits and requests documentation for future printings.

Cover and interior design by Robert Williams
Edited by Stephanie Parrish and Dave Boehi

Library of Congress Cataloging-in-Publication Data

Rainey, Dennis, 1948–
    Moments together for growing closer to God / Dennis and Barbara Rainey.
        p.   cm.
    ISBN 0-8307-3250-0
    1. Spouses—Prayer-books and devotions—English. 2. Marriage—Religious aspects—Christianity. I. Rainey, Barbara. II. Title.
    BV4596.M3R355 2003
    242'.644—dc21   2003009896

INTRODUCTION

Did you know that marriage is a spiritual relationship between you, your spouse and God? The Lord God is the Creator of marriage, and He makes it possible to build the type of relationship He and you desire. The closer you grow to God, the closer you will grow toward each other.

From the beginning of our marriage, we have resolved to build our lives and our family upon God's Word and upon daily prayer together. In Matthew 7, Jesus says that those who act upon His words "may be compared to a wise man, who built his house upon the rock. And the rain descended, and the floods came, and the winds blew, and burst against that house; and yet it did not fall, for it had been founded upon the rock" (vv. 24-25). But those who hear God's words and do not act upon them are like those who build their home on sand. "The rain descended, and the floods came, and the winds blew and burst against that house; and it fell, and great was its fall" (v. 27).

God is the head of our home, and the truth of God's Word is our home's foundation. We have found that as we make God and His Word our focus, we are able to withstand all of the trials and tribulations of life.

This devotional, *Moments Together for Growing Closer to God*, is designed to help you build your home upon the same foundation. The good news of the Bible is that the almighty God, Creator and Sustainer of the universe, actually makes it possible for us to enjoy friendship with Him. By studying His Word and praying together as a family for a few minutes each day, you can connect with God and with each other.

Each of the 30 devotionals will give you practical and biblical advice for allowing God to work in your lives as a couple and as a family. The following are some of the topics we cover:

- How praying together as a couple can transform your marriage
- Remembering your family's spiritual landmarks
- Confronting the attic of your past
- Taking advantage of your children's teachable moments
- The forgotten commandment
- Praying for your children
- Famous last words

A friendly word of warning: This is not your normal devotional! It will take you into the nitty-gritty of family relationships. It includes some strong challenges for improving your relationship with God and with each other; therefore, it probably will be one of the most valuable experiences you could have together!

Commit to spending 10 to 15 minutes each day working through these devotionals. Over the next month you will sense that the foundation of your home is getting stronger and stronger.

Dennis and Barbara Rainey

AMAZING

And they were amazed at His teaching; for He was teaching
them as one having authority, and not as the scribes.

MARK 1:22

Have you seen Jesus? I mean really seen Him? Not some kind of 900-foot-tall object but, rather, the Jesus Christ who lives in the Bible?

When I read through the book of Mark, I see a Christ who is amazing. And He obviously struck others the same when He lived on Earth.

For one thing, His teachings were amazing. The people were shaken to their core by the authority Christ had when He taught.

Second, He performed miracles that were amazing. He healed the blind, the sick, the lepers. Mark 4:35-41 gives us another little outline of a story, a brief glimpse of a miracle that Jesus performed. This is no mystical myth. This was a real event that occurred. This passage describes Jesus with His disciples and how He rebuked the wind of a storm.

On a windy day you or I could go outside and say "Hold it" to the wind. But it would just keep blowing. A wall could be built, but that really would not stop it. The wind would flow right over it. Yet Jesus turned an angry sea into a calm surface by speaking, causing the wind to stop.

Christ healed the sick, fed the 5,000 and not only walked on water but also made it possible for Peter to do the same. I sometimes wonder what it was like to be Peter as he stepped out of that boat. He had his eyes on Christ; he stepped out of the boat, and the water was solid. Then he saw the wind and began to sink.

In sermons, I've heard Peter criticized for seeing the wind and sinking—for his doubt and unbelief. But he still stepped out—he had the faith to get out of the boat *onto* the water! And he's the only person in history to walk on water, other than Jesus.

What's my point? Have you ever been amazed by His teachings? Have you ever really stepped out and taken Him at His word?

Discuss: How has God's teaching made a difference in your life?

Pray: Pray that you will see Christ as the amazing God on a daily basis.

WITH OPEN ARMS

Create in me a clean heart, O God, and renew a steadfast spirit within me. Do not cast me away from Thy presence. . . . Restore to me the joy of Thy salvation.

PSALM 51:10-12

The devil is called "the father of lies" (John 8:44)—for good reason. He will try to lead you to believe anything that will keep you from turning to God.

One of his greatest lies, I believe, is that God will reject us when we confess our sins to Him and seek to repent. Somehow we start thinking that our sins are too terrible for Him to forgive.

The truth, of course, is that God loves a contrite heart, welcomes the repentant sinner back and restores "the joy of Thy salvation." I once received a letter that underscores the power of God's forgiveness:

My wife and I have been married for six years, and together for eight. Recently I was having a lot of problems. I was unfaithful to my wife. I had fallen far from the path. She found out about the adultery and consulted a lawyer and filed for divorce.

My life was over. I didn't know what to do or where to turn. Suddenly I realized what I must do. I went to church, fell to my knees and asked God to forgive me and take over my life, set me straight. I gave it all up to Him.

Much to my surprise, He welcomed me back with open arms. I relearned how to pray and started reading the Bible. God took it from there.

This man asked his wife to attend a FamilyLife Marriage Conference with him. Reluctant at first, she finally agreed. The husband went on to write:

The Lord not only answered my prayers (by restoring my marriage) but 10 times what I had asked for! We not only did away with the lawyers and divorce papers, but we recommitted to God and each other.

Just like King David, who wrote those wonderful words in Psalm 51, this man learned that life can start anew when you are willing to approach God with a repentant heart.

Discuss: Talk about your understanding of God's forgiveness—is it absolute, total? Do you harbor any fears that God will reject you? For which sins?

Pray: If you need to confess any sins, do so now and thank God for His forgiveness.

LIFE CAN START ANEW
WHEN YOU ARE WILLING
TO APPROACH GOD
WITH A REPENTANT
HEART.

TO MIRROR GOD'S IMAGE

And God created man in His own image, in the image of
God He created him; male and female He created them.

GENESIS 1:27

Hanging in my mother's bedroom is a photograph of the Grand Teton Mountains. I gave her that 8x10-inch enlargement after photographing the Tetons from the edge of Jenny Lake.

The morning I took that picture, Jenny Lake was like a mirror. If you take the photo and turn it upside down, you can't tell which mountains are real and which are the reflection.

When I look at that picture, I think of God's first purpose for marriage: *to mirror His image.* To "mirror" God means to reflect Him; and when we reflect Him, we magnify, exalt and glorify Him. A successful marriage between two committed Christians provides a tangible model of God's love to a world that desperately needs to see who He is.

Because we're created in the image of God, people who wouldn't otherwise know what God is like should be able to look at us and get a glimpse of Him. People are never more like God than when they love one another and remain committed to each other despite their flaws.

But what happens if you toss a stone into that perfect reflection? My good friend and colleague Dave Sunde told me he once visited Jenny Lake on that same kind of clear, still day. He watched a boy skip a small stone across the placid water, immediately distorting the perfect reflection of the mountains. God's image, His reflection, is distorted when a husband or wife allows sin to enter his or her life or marriage. Your marriage represents God; protect it from the "stones"—the sin—that will distort His image.

Discuss: When people look at your marriage, how do they see an example of God's love? What would people learn about God from your marriage?

Pray: Ask God to help you keep your "mirror" polished and clear, so His image will be reflected in your marriage.

GOD'S "BOX TOP" FOR THE FAMILY

Unless the LORD builds the house, they labor in vain who build it.

PSALM 127:1

ƒor many years I taught a sixth-grade Sunday School class at our church. Each fall I would divide my class into three groups to compete in putting together a jigsaw puzzle. As these 12-year-olds scattered into three circles on the floor, I'd explain that there was only one rule in our competition: Put together the puzzle *without talking*.

The contents of one puzzle would be deposited on the floor and Group One would immediately go to work. The group would promptly set up the box top, which depicted the picture of the puzzle it was completing.

Then I would move to the second group, dump the pieces on the floor and quickly give the group a box top. What the group wouldn't know was that the box top was for another puzzle!

The third group would be given the same puzzle pieces but without a box top. Usually the kids in the group would start to protest, but I'd quickly remind them there was to be no talking!

What would follow was fascinating.

Group One would be somewhat frustrated by not being allowed to talk, but it would still make steady progress. Group Two would keep trying to use the picture, but nothing would seem to work. And since the kids in the group couldn't say anything, their frustration level would soar. The group members would look at me with pleading eyes. Soon, I'd see the wrong box top come flying out of the group!

Group Three was interesting. Because the kids had nothing to guide them, they would do their own thing. The kids would give up and just lie on the floor.

Was I a cruel teacher? No, there was a point that I was trying to make that day.

Life, marriages and families are like the pieces of the puzzle. The pieces are all there for us, but we need help to put them together.

There are a lot of competing blueprints and pictures out there vying for your commitment and mine. It only makes sense, however, to look to the God who created the family to learn a design that will work.

It's never too late to begin to use the right box top. Pull out your Bible and get started today!

Discuss: Do you think you are building your family from the right blueprints? Do you and your spouse have the same box top? If you continue on your current path, what will your home look like?

Pray: Ask God to give you discernment to recognize whether or not you are building your marriage with the wrong box top.

NO FAULT, NO RESPONSIBILITY

He who created them from the beginning made
them male and female, and said, "For this cause a man
shall leave his father and mother, and shall cleave to his wife;
and the two shall become one flesh."

MATTHEW 19:4-5

Hundreds of thousands of marriages are dissolved each year in the courtrooms of our land under relatively recent laws that allow no-fault divorce. This is the thoroughly modern and practical way for two people to wash their hands of a marriage and terminate all responsibility to one another.

It's cleaner, faster and easier than in the old days, when the courts attempted to establish responsibility for the breakup of the marriage. Now, if no one is at fault, no one can be blamed. If neither party was wrong or wronged and both want out of the relationship, then shouldn't two people be allowed to dissolve their relationship?

It all sounds perfectly rational, but it should raise questions for Christians. Marriage was established by God for our good and His glory. Marriage occurs because of a covenant between a man, a woman and God. If in our minds accountability is removed, then marriage vows are reduced to meaningless words. Commitments become conditional, temporal bargains.

Furthermore, if it's no one's fault that the marriage failed, are we also saying it is no one's responsibility to make the marriage work? The permanence of my marriage vows to Barbara motivates me to be responsible for the health of our relationship. It's for life—no excuses.

A society that allows for no-fault divorce cannot escape the long-term consequences of its no-responsibility marriages. Most people will say they believe in marriage. The facts suggest that our society believes in marriage the same way Zsa Zsa Gabor does; she allegedly said, after she married and divorced for the eighth time, that she really did believe in marriage.

Someone is *at fault* here. The cure for our nation's divorce epidemic is a vaccine of biblical accountability and godly responsibility to keep our covenants, vows and commitments.

Discuss: Tell your spouse today that you'd marry him or her all over again. Reaffirm your love and commitment by telling him or her, "It's still 'til death do us part!"

Pray: Ask God to help you model the kind of commitment and responsibility that will communicate

to your children and to the world the permanence
of marriage and its vows.

THE PERMANENCE OF MY
MARRIAGE VOWS MOTIVATES ME
TO BE RESPONSIBLE FOR THE
HEALTH OF OUR RELATIONSHIP.
IT'S FOR LIFE—NO EXCUSES.

PRAYING WITH BARBARA

*Behold, how good and how pleasant it is for brothers
to dwell together in unity! It is like the dew of Hermon,
coming down upon the mountains of Zion; for there the
LORD commanded the blessing—life forever.*

PSALM 133:1,3

Barbara and I, early in our marriage, started the habit of praying together before we went to sleep. If there is one simple ritual I would urge couples to begin adopting in their marriages, it is this one—the habit of praying together every day.

For us, this habit of acknowledging God's presence in our lives and marriage has, I believe, saved us from many nights of isolation. Nightly prayer keeps us from building walls between each other. And it builds bridges across chasms that have widened between us during the day.

It isn't always easy, though. I can remember one occasion where we ended up in bed facing in opposite directions. I didn't want to pray with her. But in my heart Jesus Christ was asking me, *Are you going to pray with her tonight?*

"I don't like her tonight, Lord."

I know you don't. But you're the one who tells people that you pray with your wife all the time.

"Yes, Lord. But you know, Lord, she's 80 percent wrong."

But your 20 percent started the whole thing, God reminded me.

Slowly but surely, at the Lord's nudging, I turned over and said, "Sweetheart, will you forgive me?" And we talked and prayed.

I don't know about you, but we just can't seem to pray if we're out of fellowship with each other. I thank God for that little tradition that He helped us build early in our marriage.

Discuss: For a week, commit yourself to praying with your mate before you go to bed each night. At the end of the week, ask yourselves if your relationship has changed as a result.

Pray: Perhaps you need to pray this prayer first: "Lord, teach me how to pray with my spouse. I'm afraid."

THIS HABIT OF
ACKNOWLEDGING GOD'S
PRESENCE IN OUR LIVES AND
MARRIAGE HAS SAVED US FROM
MANY NIGHTS OF ISOLATION.

WHEN LITTLE EQUALS MUCH

He who is faithful in a very little thing is faithful also in much.

LUKE 16:10

What would happen in our homes if we saw an epidemic in which husbands and wives were infected with faithfulness in little things? What if we really did all the little things we say we'll do?

Many people these days want the "much" without the "very little." We want the tip without the toil, the gain without the grind, the sweets without the sweat, the prize without the pain, the perks without the perseverance. Duty, diligence, hard work and attention to details are rare commodities in any endeavor—whether at home, at work or at church.

How about cheering your family members on when

- a good deed is done for someone when no one is apparently watching;
- your husband is honest in preparing your family's income tax return;

- your spouse stands up for the truth at work, regardless of the consequences;
- a mother is faithfully taking the time to rear the next generation (so much of her work is unseen and unappreciated by others);
- a child tells the truth instead of lying, even when lying would be easier.

How do you view the little things? As nitpicky things to be ignored or that get in your way? Or as stepping-stones to receiving the true riches of the Kingdom?

What would happen to the next generation if we trained our children to be faithful in little things as well as in what the world considers much—intelligence, wealth and athletic ability? If they don't learn from you to be faithful in the little things, then what kinds of leaders, workers, husbands, wives, fathers and mothers will they make?

If you don't teach them, who will?

Discuss: Why is faithfulness in little things so important in a marriage? In a family? How can you impart this truth to your family?

Pray: Ask God to build your character by enabling you to be faithful in little things with your spouse and your family.

WHAT'S GROWING IN YOUR GARDEN?

(PART ONE)

Then the LORD passed by in front of him and proclaimed,
"The LORD, the LORD God, compassionate and gracious,
slow to anger, and abounding in lovingkindness and
truth . . . yet He will by no means leave the guilty unpun-
ished, visiting the iniquity of fathers on the children and on
the grandchildren to the third and fourth generations."

EXODUS 34:6-7

$\mathcal{D}$ag Hammarskjöld, former secretary-general of the
United Nations, once said,

> You cannot play with the animal in you without
> becoming wholly animal, play with falsehood with-
> out forfeiting your right to truth, play with cruelty
> without losing your sensitivity of mind. He who
> wants to keep his garden tidy doesn't reserve a plot
> for weeds.[1]

Did you know that what you grow and cultivate in your
garden today could spread to your offspring? Did you know

that a sin you now tolerate could still be tormenting your great-grandchildren in the year 2140? That's four generations from now.

Consider the warning of Exodus 34:6-7. What does it mean? Why would God establish a system that visits one generation's sins on three or four other generations?

I have a hunch that God is trying to tell us that the way we live impacts others and is of supreme importance to Him. Possibly He's using a warning of future judgment on our descendants to keep us on the straight and narrow today.

Whether you like it or not, your children are becoming just like you. Their little eyes are watching to see how you relate to your mate, how you pray and how you walk with Christ on a daily basis. They hear your words and subconsciously mimic your attitudes, actions and even your mannerisms.

And as time goes by, you'll find that they've inherited some of the same tendencies toward sin that you learned from your own parents. That's why, for example, so many children from broken homes grow up and fail in their own marriages.

Your kids will grow up to be like you. Is that a sobering thought or an encouraging one?

Discuss: In what ways do you want your children to be like you? In what ways do you not want them to be like you?

Pray: Is there a sin in your life that you've tolerated? Go to God in prayer right now and confess it. As you repent, you may want to ask God for grace to protect your children from that sin in the future.

Note

1. Dag Hammarskjöld, *Markings* (New York: Alfred A. Knopf, 1964), p. 15.

WHETHER YOU LIKE IT OR NOT, YOUR CHILDREN ARE BECOMING JUST LIKE YOU.

WHAT'S GROWING IN YOUR GARDEN?
(PART TWO)

*But showing love to a thousand generations of those
who love me and keep my commandments.*

DEUTERONOMY 5:10 (*NIV*)

I'll be honest with you: The thought of my kids sinning in
the same areas that I sin has bolstered my obedience to God.
I'm reminded of the piercing statement by C. H. Spurgeon,
"Sin would have fewer takers if its consequences occurred
immediately."

Just think for a moment of the sins that could be visited upon your children. With what do you struggle? Lust?
Selfishness? Anger? Lack of discipline? Jealousy? Pride? How
about deceit? Broken promises? A gossiping tongue?

The twenty-first century could be a scary time to be
alive. I wonder how the sins of adultery, divorce and addic-
tion will affect future generations.

So what are we to do? Wallow in guilt because we are far
from perfect? Are we enslaved to our ancestors' wrong choices and, thus, permanently subject to the punishment of God?

No, we can break the chain through our repentance and confession. God in His grace stands ready to forgive us and grant us favor. You can, by faith, stop even the most tyrannical control of a sin that has beset your family for generations.

The good news is that God also gives us a wonderful promise: Your righteousness can still be influencing others a thousand generations from now. That's encouraging!

One of our FamilyLife staff members is committed to breaking the chains of sin from his past. When speaking to individuals considering vocational Christian ministry, he always says, "I grew up in a broken home and I don't want to end up like my father. He lived his life for himself, and at his funeral there were only 10 people in attendance. I want a packed funeral—full of people my life has impacted. I want to leave a heritage that will outlast me."

Discuss: What type of faith would you like your children and grandchildren to have?

Pray: Ask God to protect your life, marriage and family from sin. Ask Him to enable you to leave a legacy of righteousness to a thousand generations.

YOUR RIGHTEOUSNESS CAN
STILL BE INFLUENCING OTHERS
A THOUSAND GENERATIONS
FROM NOW.

CATCHING A GLIMPSE

*I have no greater joy than this, to hear of my
children walking in the truth.*

3 JOHN 4

The Rainey Thanksgiving Brunch is a time when we emphasize thanking God for how He has worked in our lives. Over the years, it's been interesting—and gratifying—to hear what our kids have expressed.

One year our daughter Rebecca wrote,

I'm thankful for being able to have a family. I'm thankful to have a big sister. I'm thankful for being able to be a part of God's family. I'm thankful for being able to learn. I'm thankful for Dad's sixth-grade Sunday School class.

Here's what Benjamin, then a senior in high school, wrote:

1. I'm thankful for God in my life and the things He has given me to be thankful for.
2. Samuel's friendship.

3. Mom and Dad and the example they set of how to live a godly life.
4. My ministry at my high school and my sisters and all they've taught me about relationships.

And Samuel, then 15, had this to say:

1. I'm thankful that Ashley can come home. [This was her first year away at college and we were all thrilled that she was home.]
2. My family.
3. My muscular dystrophy and my trip to Mayo Clinic.
4. *I got to shoot a deer.*
5. A great brother.

It was special to hear our kids thank God for each other as well as for hardships in their lives—Samuel had only learned the previous summer that he had MD. After all the conflicts the kids had had over the years, Barbara and I could finally see them starting to come together.

Parenting is a long and relentless task. You often wonder whether you are succeeding or failing, and you may not know the results of your efforts for many years. So when you catch just a glimpse that your kids are "walking in the truth," you can't help but rejoice.

Our heavenly Father rejoices over the growth in our lives with even greater intensity than we rejoice over our children's. He also rejoices when we thank Him for the many gifts that He has given us.

Discuss: What evidence do you have that God is working in your life or in the lives of your family? Write the evidence down so that you won't forget it.

Pray: Thank God for a right choice that you, your spouse or your child has recently made.

A DAY OF REST

You shall work six days, but on the seventh day you shall rest; even during plowing time and harvest you shall rest.

EXODUS 34:21

Within the Ten Commandments, God has provided a long-standing truth that our modern culture is ignoring, to its detriment: the Sabbath. The Sabbath is to be a day set apart for God—a day of rest in which to refuel our perspectives and refresh our communion with Him.

God knows that after working hard for six days, we all need some time off. The problem is, we ignore His command and race through life. But our need for rest can't be denied. Which word best describes our lives and our society: "rest" or "weariness"?

God knew that it's important to step out of the demands of work and the pace of everyday life. That is the purpose of the Sabbath—to give us time to rest, to reflect, to think critically about life and where our choices are taking us.

Over the last five years, Barbara and I became more aware of our need to regard the Sabbath as a day of rest. And I'd have to say that we feel like we have a long way to go to really recapture what God had in mind. But we try to make

Sunday different. A nap. Time to read. Recreation as a family that is not demanding. We usually do not work in the yard. (The kids now remind us of the Sabbath if we ask them to do something outside on Sunday!) And Barbara and I generally go out on a date to eat dinner and talk on Sunday evening.

Now, let me make one thing real clear—we don't always do a great job of observing the day of rest. Barbara would join me in saying that occasionally we fail miserably, but the standard is there and we are moving toward it in our choices about how we spend our time.

If we in the Christian community would decide to rest on Sundays, we would begin to reap the enriching qualities of clear minds and relaxed spirits and the knowledge that our lives are pleasing to God.

Discuss: How do you spend your Sundays? What can you change in your schedule to begin to make Sunday a day of rest?

Pray: Pray that you will take the time God has set aside to gain the rest you need to face the pressures and responsibilities of your life.

GOD KNOWS THAT
AFTER WORKING HARD
FOR SIX DAYS, WE ALL NEED
SOME TIME OFF.

DEFENSES AGAINST THE LION

Be of sober spirit, be on the alert. Your adversary, the devil, prowls about like a roaring lion, seeking someone to devour.
1 PETER 5:8

I've found a widespread misconception about Satan's efforts to devour us by presenting us with temptations. Many people think that it's a sin just to be tempted. The fact is, being tempted is normal for a Christian—especially one who is growing.

Even Christ, we recall, was tempted in that classic confrontation with the devil at the beginning of His ministry. *Giving in* to temptation is the problem.

So how can we resist the roaring lion? First, *know your weaknesses.* If temptation occurs when you are alone, build in some safeguards. Ask your spouse to keep you honest and accountable by asking the hard questions that you don't want anyone to ask you (for example, Did you watch any provocative movies in your hotel room on your recent business trip?). Keep your mind focused, and prepare for times when you are alone by setting some boundaries. Or the next time you are tempted, call your mate and ask him or her to pray with you and for you.

Second, *draw upon His power to stand firm*. As Paul says, "God will not allow us to be tempted beyond what we can withstand, if we rely on His strength to deliver us" (see 1 Cor. 10:13). Talk to God about the temptation and ask Him to help you stand firm.

Third, if you are toying with a temptation, *realize that you might as well be handling a serpent*. Some people stand as close to the edge of sin as they can, thinking they are above it, when they may actually be toying with the death of their marriages, their family relationships and their ministries. Paul counsels, "If you think you are standing firm, be careful that you don't fall!" (see 1 Cor. 10:12).

I received a phone call from a man who was about to lose his marriage and job because he crossed the line in his job. I wish you could have listened to the agony that was in his life because of his compromise. Let me encourage and exhort you to live a holy life and resist the temptations that are set before you.

Discuss: Are you crossing the line or standing anywhere near a danger point right now? If so, confess your sins so that you may be free.

Pray: Ask God to teach you how to stand firm in the spiritual battle. Call on the Holy Spirit and His indwelling power to give you the strength to stand firm.

THE FACT IS,
BEING TEMPTED IS NORMAL
FOR A CHRISTIAN—ESPECIALLY
ONE WHO IS GROWING.

AIRBRUSH CHRISTIANS

Therefore, confess your sins to one another, and pray
for one another, so that you may be healed.

JAMES 5:16

Oliver Cromwell, the British statesman, war hero and leader of the British Isles, posed for a portrait one day. He commissioned the painter to paint him "warts and all." Cromwell was willing to be known for who he really was; he was not trying to hide.

I don't think his story typifies the kind of airbrush society in which we live. Today you can take an unflattering photograph of yourself and have all the "warts" removed. They will fix your lumpy nose, change the color of your eyes, improve your smile and remove any unsightly blemishes—all with either an airbrush or with computer enhancement!

We are a culture of fake people: airbrushing our lives, creating illusions, never willing to admit our faults to others. And this is often just as true of Christians. Once you know how to talk and relate to other Christians, it's often easy to give them the impression that you are much more mature in Christ than you really are.

The irony is that true maturity begins to occur when you are willing to confess your sins to others. We're often afraid to be so vulnerable, and yet people always seem to respond with warmth and understanding.

As James 5:16 says, healing occurs when you come to the point in your walk with God that you know you won't get rid of sin by concealing it; you need to become accountable within the Body of Christ. When we confess our sins to God and to others, then little by little we become like Jesus Christ.

Perhaps there is no better relationship than marriage for two people to begin to experience authenticity. In marriage there's no airbrushing faults and removing blemishes; it's life—up close and personal—just like God intended it.

Discuss: Are you concealing any sins that you need to confess, first to God and then to others?

Pray: Ask God to conform you to His image as you make yourself more accountable to others in the Body of Christ—particularly your spouse.

FRIENDSHIPS WITH OTHER WOMEN

BY BARBARA RAINEY

Finally, brethren, rejoice, be made complete,
be comforted, be like-minded.

2 CORINTHIANS 13:11

In my relationship with Dennis, I am confident that he understands me, my role and my struggles. We have spent endless hours talking together to create this rapport. He has been with me through many difficult times. He has been a substitute mother to the children when I've been out of the house, so he knows a great deal about that role and its responsibilities.

But there is a point beyond which he cannot go. Only another wife and mother can really share the pain I felt in childbirth, my struggles with understanding my role in marriage or the feeling that I'm just a need machine, designed solely to meet the needs of others. Only women can join with me in prayer about issues like these. Only other mothers can provide the support and motivation I need to carry the daily burdens involved in bringing up children.

I need a deep affinity with two or three women, and I have it. It's wonderful. I am affirmed every time we talk by phone, get together or correspond. And when I feel good about myself, Dennis feels less pressure to try to meet all of my needs.

May I urge you, men, to encourage your wife to find at least one woman with whom she can identify? This friendship should not take your place as her primary source of approval, but it can supplement the self-image you are helping her build.

Here's another tip: Give your wife a weekend off to get away for a retreat with a friend. On Sunday evening, your wife will return with a better perspective about herself. She'll be encouraged and built up in ways that you as a man could never accomplish. This retreat is especially needed if your wife is occupied with young children or works outside the home, thus having little time to develop friendships.

Dennis and I encourage you to resist the tendency to be threatened by your wife's friendships with women. Give her time and encouragement to develop these friendships. You'll never regret it.

Discuss: Discuss your wife's friendships. Does she have too few? Too many? Are they the right kind? Does she have enough time to pursue them? What are her friendship needs in the stage of life that she's in right now?

Pray: Ask God to give your wife at least one female soul mate who can identify with her season of life.

SPIRITUAL LANDMARKS

And he said to the sons of Israel, "When your children ask
their fathers in time to come, saying, 'What are these stones?'
then you shall inform your children, saying, 'Israel crossed
this Jordan on dry ground.' For the LORD your God dried up
the waters of the Jordan before you until you had crossed, . . .
that all the peoples of the earth may know that
the hand of the LORD is mighty."

JOSHUA 4:21-24

If you've traveled around the United States, you've noticed
historical landmarks. In Williamsburg, Virginia, they have
restored a community that was very significant in the
founding of our country. When you sit where our founding
fathers sat, you feel a sense of the events that took place
there.

Landmarks like these remind us of our heritage as Ameri-
cans.

I find it significant that God gave the Israelites landmarks as well. These landmarks caused the people to remember Him and His provisions for them.

Joshua 4 tells of a spiritual landmark that symbolized
the provision of God. One man from each tribe took a stone

from the middle of the Jordan River and together they created a memorial. Why do you think God directed them to do that? I think it's because we are forgetful, and children are curious.

Children ask great questions: "How big is high?" "How far away is a star?" I can almost picture a grandfather walking with his grandson in Gilgal near the Jordan River. The little boy, seeing that pile of stones, asks, "Grandpa, why are these stones here?"

"Well, let me tell you about that. . . ."

And when the story is over: "Aw, come on, Grandpa. You've got to be kidding me. The river stopped—in flood season? It was dry ground?"

"Well, how do *you* think the stones got here?"

Spiritual landmarks were designed by God to remind us of how He provided for His people in the past and to prompt us to believe Him today.

Discuss: What are some landmarks in your life? What are some ways God has worked in your life? Let me encourage you both to take a sheet of paper and list the major spiritual landmarks in your lives.

Pray: Why not find a place where you can pile some stones together to remind you of something significant God has done in your life? Pile up the stones and then celebrate God's provision by giving thanks together.

ENTERING THE ATTIC
(PART ONE)

*There is no fear in love; but perfect love
cast out fear, because fear involves punishment, and
the one who fears is not perfected in love.*

1 JOHN 4:18

As a young boy growing up in a small, white two-story frame home, I was terrified of the attic. An eerie stillness enveloped me as I ventured into this windowless, hot, creepy room. The scent of mothballs perfumed the air. Invisible threads of spider webs attempted to capture me if I got too near. Mysterious shapes covered by sheets and blankets crouched in corners, casting suspicious shadows on the plank floor.

I just knew that the attic contained more than discarded junk. Something was living up there, something that would mercilessly defend its territory against pint-sized trespassers. I never saw this creature, but I knew it was there.

Everyone has an attic in his or her mind. It may be a room in which past mistreatment is stored. Memories of when you failed others or when others failed you may haunt and accuse you. Whatever shaped your self-image as you grew up—praise and encouragement or relentless criticism—is in your attic.

Although I feared going into the attic alone, with a companion I became downright courageous. That dark scary spot in my home then became little more than just another room.

You and your mate can be that kind of companion for each other. One or both of you may be extremely fearful of visiting the attic of your past, but if you enter it together, you can give each other the encouragement and strength to seek God's perspective on these past events. Take a moment and think of ways that you can be a supportive friend who helps your mate enter the attic and face down negative role models that may be lurking there.

Remember that God will meet the two of you there in the attic—you will not be alone.

Discuss: Is the attic of your past fearful or inviting? If the past creates emotional turmoil in your life, what can your mate do to help you courageously face your fears?

Pray: Ask God to help you and your mate exhibit the love of Christ to one another and help each other conquer fear as you build a home without a frightening attic.

ENTERING THE ATTIC
(PART TWO)

*I press on toward the goal for the prize of the
upward call of God in Christ Jesus.*

PHILIPPIANS 3:14

I have five suggestions for helping your mate dig through
the attic of the past and focus on the future:

1. *Work with your spouse to get the problem fully on the
   table.* Talk about how your parents treated you
   and ask your mate to share his or her experiences. Be patient. Talking about these things can
   be very painful. Affirm and strengthen your
   mate by listening and by expressing your own
   acceptance.
2. *Help your mate understand his or her parents.* Talk
   together about them and put their lives in prop-
   er perspective. Remind your mate that his or her
   parents probably did the best they could.
3. *Give your mate the perspective that God's grace and
   power are greater than his or her parents' mistakes.* No
   matter how bad a person's home life was, God
   delights in resurrecting damaged self-images

and restoring dignity to such people. Talk about the overwhelming power of grace, and express your confidence and belief in the greatness of God's love and acceptance.

4. *Encourage your mate to forgive his or her parents—completely.* You may need to first talk this out as a couple. A qualified counselor may be needed if you feel you cannot help your mate resolve this emotionally charged issue and forgive his or her parents.

5. *Help your mate determine how he or she will respond to his or her parents.* Your spouse has no control over how he or she was treated as a child, but he or she does have control over how he or she will relate to them today. Help your spouse focus on what his or her parents did right, and how you both are the benefactors. Help your spouse think of ways that he or she can honor his or her parents.

In some cases, it may take months or years for all the hurt to be brought out into the open. But if you're patient and if you and your mate are willing to allow Jesus Christ to be Lord of this relationship, healing is possible.

Discuss: What is a tangible way to forgive your parents?

Pray: If appropriate, tell God that you are willing to forgive and love your parents.

GOD'S GRACE AND POWER
ARE GREATER THAN OUR
PARENTS' MISTAKES.

WEAK ENOUGH FOR GRACE

BY BARBARA RAINEY

*My grace is sufficient for you, for power
is perfected in weakness.*

2 CORINTHIANS 12:9

When I learned that God had decided to add a sixth child
to our brood, I was completely caught off guard. I was sick
physically, drained mentally and tired just thinking about six
children. After two months of internal stuggle, I was encouraged through Isaiah 41:10 that God had chosen to give me
this new child and that He would also give me the strength
and help I needed. He enabled me to accept His will.

Through that experience I also learned to be more tol-
erant of my humanity. I discovered that I often want—and
expect—instant maturity. I often forget that I'm only human
and that it's just that kind of human weakness that God's
grace is designed for.

It's little wonder that in our humanity it can be hard to
see God's will for our lives. His plan for us is much like
a quilt: There is an overall pattern, or design, made up of

hundreds of pieces. Since we lack God's overall perspective, it shouldn't surprise us to wonder what this or that dark-colored piece is doing in the quilt.

Sometimes the marriage relationship becomes one of those pieces whose place in the larger pattern is hard to see. Even the most intimate couples often find that it can take time to work out areas of disagreement. We should not expect less in our relationship with our heavenly Father. Becoming conformed to His will takes time; it's a process.

Yet by faith I affirm that God is the Creative Designer of my life. He sees an award-winning masterpiece. With that trust, I can rely on His plan, knowing that His grace gives me time to conform to His will when the pieces I see are not of my choosing.

Discuss: Talk about ways you've seen each other grow in the past five years. Then share what you think God is doing in your life today.

Pray: Ask God for confidence in Him, knowing that the overall pattern of your life will give you rest to quiet the questions you have about individual pieces. Thank Him for giving us grace that is greater than our struggles.

GOD'S PLAN FOR US IS MUCH
LIKE A QUILT: THERE'S AN
OVERALL PATTERN MADE UP OF
HUNDREDS OF PIECES.

IS THERE A MINISTER IN THE HOUSE?

An elder must be blameless, the husband of but one wife,
a man whose children believe and are not open to the
charge of being wild and disobedient.

TITUS 1:6 (NIV)

Is there a minister at your house? The apostle Paul wanted elders in the church who could also minister the gospel to their own households.

When I suggest to fathers that they are to be ministers to their families, they tend to shy away, thinking I mean they have to be accomplished theologians and do a lot of eloquent praying before meals. But that's not what being a family minister is all about.

By being there and making your family a priority, you'll find plenty of opportunities to minister to your children by showing them what's really important in life. I'm learning to take advantage of the teachable moments—moments when my kids are open to spiritual truth.

Years ago I was cuddled up next to our daughter Ashley on the lower bunk at bedtime. Somehow we found ourselves discussing the second coming of Christ. I told her, "Yes, Jesus is coming back; and He's going to take all those with Jesus in their hearts with Him, and it's going to be fantastic."

Ashley had received Christ, but she wondered about her brother Benjamin. "When it comes time for him to invite Jesus into his heart, he'll do that," I said.

Benjamin was lying in the upper bunk, and he popped his head over the edge. "Dad, tomorrow would you tell me how to invite Jesus into my heart?" he asked.

So the next day he, too, made a profession of faith. And his very next words were, "Daddy, could we play ball?"

I couldn't know at that time whether Benjamin had made a true, life-changing commitment to Christ. But the fact was that when he was interested, I was there.

Discuss: As a father, do you find it difficult to discuss spiritual matters with your family? In what other ways can you minister to your family? Have you found a good time, such as bedtime, for having heart-to-heart conversations?

Pray: Pray that you will be able to embody the essentials of being a minister, especially just by being there, in your family life.

THE GREATEST POWER

In the fear of the LORD there is strong confidence,
and His children will have refuge.

PROVERBS 14:26

As a parent you know that no matter what you do to raise your children, God is ultimately in control of their lives. You want them to walk with Him and have "strong confidence" in Him.

The greatest power you have is to pray for your children. But how should you pray?

First, *pray that God will teach your children*. I'll never forget when two of our kids were having a conflict. We tried everything—rewards, punishments, threats—but nothing worked. Finally we said, "Okay, Lord, we'll pray."

For two nights we prayed. On the second night, one child in the conflict had a dream that the other child had died. He came to us and said, "I was sad I'd treated him so badly." The problems stopped, just like that. In one night, God changed what we hadn't been able to change in weeks.

Second, *pray that you'll catch your kids when they do evil*. You know what it's like: One of your children is lying or stealing or manipulating others, but you haven't been able to catch him in the act. Pray, "Lord, help me catch this kid. Give me some evidence." I've knelt beside the bed of a child we couldn't catch and laid my hands on him and prayed, "Lord, You know the truth in this matter. If this child is lying, I pray You'll help me catch him."

Does God answer these prayers? You bet He does. I think God has compassion upon the helpless parent!

Third, *pray with your children*. Get down next to their cheeks, cuddle and pray. Pray for the important things going on in their lives, and pray for their futures—that they will walk with God, marry a godly spouse, etc. They love it. And so does God.

Discuss: What do you want God to teach your children? Write down at least two items for each child.

Pray: Ask God to give you wisdom as you raise your children and to help you to catch them if they stray from what is right. Ask Him to teach them so that they grow in wisdom.

BIG LITTLE WORDS

Death and life are in the power of the tongue,
and those who love it will eat its fruit.

PROVERBS 18:21

A friend recently showed me a Hallmark card with these words beautifully scripted on the outside: "If you love something, set it free. If it returns, you haven't lost it. If it disappears and never comes back, then it wasn't truly yours to begin with."

Inside, the thought continued: "and if it just sits there watching television unaware that it's been set free, you probably already married it."

Cute words like that bring a smile to my face. But there are other words that can bring pain, guilt and shame. As Proverbs 18:21 says, your remarks, your words, can bring life or death.

I recall, as a young lad, going with my dad to the ice house to get block ice for making homemade ice cream. The iceman knew exactly how to use his pick to strike the ice and break off a smaller block of just the right size.

In the family, your tongue can be like an ice pick chipping away at another's self-worth and character. I've counseled people who knew their mates' weak spots and who, in stressful moments, would use words to purposely hack, slice and cut their partners.

But the tongue can also be used as beautifully as a paintbrush. Years ago, before we started our family, Barbara amazed me with her ability to paint; she can cause a beautiful picture to emerge on a previously blank canvas. In a similar way, your words can encourage the image of Christ to appear in the lives of each member of your family. With words of respect and kindness you can elicit the beauty in a person.

Discuss: What are some words that had a positive influence on you as you grew up? What are some that had a negative influence? In what areas or circumstances do you need to watch the words you say to your mate? And to your children?

Pray: If appropriate, confess any words that you have used to tear down your spouse or family. Ask God to empower you to use your tongue to build up your spouse and each family member.

THE FORGOTTEN COMMANDMENT

Honor your father and your mother.

EXODUS 20:12

Honoring your parents is a command for children of all ages. There is no exception clause in this command that exempts the adult child from responsibility.

I can almost sense you starting to squirm in your seat. Honoring your parents seems risky.

Let me take a few moments to tell you what honoring your parents is—and what it isn't.

Honoring your parents does not mean endorsing irresponsibility or sin. It is not a denial of what they have done wrong as parents. It does not mean you flatter them by "emotionally stuffing" the mistakes they've made or denying the emotional or even the physical pain they may have caused you.

Since you are an adult child, honoring your parents will not place you back under their authority. It does not give them permission to manipulate you. It doesn't mean crawling back into the cradle and becoming a helpless child again.

Honoring your parents means choosing to place great value on your relationship with them.

Honoring your parents means taking the initiative to improve the relationship.

Honoring your parents means obeying them until you establish yourself as an adult.

Honoring your parents means recognizing what they've done right in your life.

Honoring your parents means recognizing the sacrifices they have made for you.

Honoring your parents means praising them for the legacy they have passed on to you.

Honoring your parents means seeing them through the eyes of Christ, with understanding and compassion.

Honoring your parents means forgiving them as Christ has forgiven you.

It is an attitude accompanied by actions that say to your parents, "You are worthy. You have value. You are the person God sovereignly placed in my life."

Discuss: What did your parents do right as they raised you? What steps can you take to improve your relationship with your parents?

Pray: Ask God to empower you through the Holy Spirit to take one step toward honoring your parents.

HONORING YOUR PARENTS
IS AN ATTITUDE ACCOMPANIED
BY ACTIONS THAT SAYS,
"YOU ARE WORTHY. YOU HAVE
VALUE. YOU ARE THE PERSON
GOD SOVEREIGNLY PLACED
IN MY LIFE."

PRIMING THE POSITIVE PUMP

Grace and peace to you from God our Father and the Lord Jesus Christ. I thank my God every time I remember you.

PHILIPPIANS 1:2-3 (*NIV*)

I wonder how many of us thank God every time we remember our parents? Almost everyone has negative memories of their childhood, but there seems to be an epidemic of parent blaming these days. I want to suggest a way to balance this negativity with positive memories of your home.

In case it's hard to get these positive thoughts flowing, here are some pump primers. (You might want to answer several of these while on a date with your spouse.)

- Where did your parents take you on vacation, and what did you do?
- What did you most enjoy doing with your dad? With your mom?
- What smells today remind you of Dad and Mom?
- What was your favorite room in your house?
- What was your favorite family tradition?
- What were the family jokes?

- What special phrases or nicknames did your family invent?
- What was your favorite Christmas? Your favorite birthday?
- What problems did your parents help you through when you were a teenager?
- What did other people think about your parents?
- What values from your childhood home are you trying to pass on to your children?

As you think about these questions, thank God for the positive memories and the power they have to give your own home strength and stability. You may want to write some of your thoughts down and, if possible, send them in a letter—or perhaps a more formal tribute—to your parents. It's a practical and tangible way to let them know you wish them "grace and peace."

Discuss: Spend some time answering the above questions.

Pray: Pray that you will be able to incorporate the strongest positive memories from your childhood home into your own family life.

KEEPING YOUR FOCUS CLEAR

*But when Cephas came to Antioch, I opposed him
to his face, because he stood condemned.*

GALATIANS 2:11

$\mathcal{T}$his famous confrontation between Paul and Peter occurred without rupturing their relationship. Paul was able to focus on the issue at hand. He didn't use it as an opportunity to bring up other problems he may have had with Peter, and he didn't try to assassinate Peter's character.

Here are some ways to follow Paul's example to keep your focus clear during confrontations:

1. *Stick to one issue.* Don't save up a series of complaints and let your mate have them all at once. If you find yourself saying "And another thing . . . ," then you know you are getting off track.

2. *Focus on behavior rather than character.* Confrontation must not turn into character assassination. Let's say you need to talk about sticking to a budget. Discuss available finances and necessary

expenses, instead of calling your mate a spend-thrift. Avoid attacking the person, and remember to use "I" language. Say, "I think we can keep from going in the hole each month by . . . ," not "You always drain us dry before the end of the month!"

3. *Focus on the facts rather than the motives.* Your teenager forgot to tell you what time the school function would be over. Say, "I worry about you when you aren't here when I expect you," not "You just don't care about anyone but yourself!"

4. *Above all, keep your focus on understanding each other rather than on who is winning or losing.* Listen carefully to what the other person says. See if some other issue is really at stake in the disagreement.

A healthy relationship with God is open to His gentle confrontation—it does not try to sweep difficulties under the rug. In the same way, healthy families face conflicts openly. It is best when the focus of confrontation is clear and the overall goal is to create a family climate in which everyone is a winner. As with the difficulty between Paul and Peter, clearer focus can lead to family unity, not isolation.

Discuss: Think of any feeling of frustration you may have right now about your family. Are a multitude of issues the cause, or is there a single root problem?

Pray: Ask God to give you clear insight into the needs and feelings of every member of your family as well as a sharper focus on family issues.

A CONFRONTATION REWARDED

*But if you return to Me and keep My commandments
and do them, though those of you who have been scattered
were in the most remote part of the heavens, I will gather
them from there and will bring them to the place where
I have chosen to cause My name to dwell.*

NEHEMIAH 1:9

The book of Nehemiah may seem like an unlikely source
for advice to families, but it contains five important guide-
lines for confrontation from which couples can learn.

Jerusalem had been destroyed, and most of God's people were in Babylonian captivity. Nehemiah wanted to take
a group back to Jerusalem to rebuild the city, but he first
had to confront King Artaxerxes to gain permission.
Nehemiah's model for facing problems consisted of five
principles you can apply in your own life:

1. *He took time to pray* (see Neh. 1:4-11; 2:4). Most
   problems can be solved when you get together,
   take the issue before the Lord and let Him calm

you down a bit before you actually begin to talk.

2. *Nehemiah expressed loyalty, encouragement and support* before raising the issue at hand. He opened his conversation with the king by saying, "Let the king live forever!" (2:3). To apply this concept to confrontation, affirm each other and create a climate of trust, so your mate can hear what you need to say.

3. *Nehemiah was truthful.* He came right out with the problem, telling the king that the walls of Jerusalem were in rubble and that the few Israelites who had survived were in great danger. Be truthful with your spouse about the real problem. Glossing over sin is deceitful.

4. *Nehemiah had an attitude of submission.* He let the king know that he was not only interested in the fate of Jerusalem but in the king's interests as well. Confrontation should benefit both spouses, not just one.

5. *Nehemiah was specific in his request.* He asked the king for letters to take him safely on his journey and for materials to rebuild the walls of Jerusalem (see 2:7-8). Do you know what you need from your spouse to resolve your problem? Be specific.

Homes can be built (or rebuilt) through healthy confrontation.

Discuss: Think about past confrontations. Which of the five principles above could have helped you?

Pray: Pray that God will help you balance personal honesty with sensitivity to others.

BE TRUTHFUL WITH YOUR
SPOUSE ABOUT THE REAL
PROBLEM. GLOSSING OVER
SIN IS DECEITFUL.

FAILURE AND FORGIVENESS

Be kind to one another, tender-hearted, forgiving each other,
just as God in Christ also has forgiven you.

EPHESIANS 4:32

*F*ailures at home come in all sorts of sizes, shapes and weights.

There are the small failures called mistakes, errors or goofs: breaking a piece of china; spilling catsup on a new shirt; ripping your jeans; while wearing golf shoes, stepping on your wife's foot; failing to carry out the garbage.

There are the heavier, medium-sized packages of failure that hurt a little deeper: shouting at the kids for the fourth time in one day, saying something hurtful to your spouse, habitually promising something to your kids and then going back on your promise.

Then there are the cumbersome and heaviest of failures that leave us feeling crushed under the weight: a divorce, unfaithfulness, an estranged relationship, a rebellious teenager who thinks he is always right, physical or verbal abuse, the failure to lead your wife and children spiritually.

How can families deal with big and little failures?

First, I think *we've got to be truthful about our sins*. The Bible calls this confession. When we confess a sin, it means we agree with God concerning that sin and turn from it.

I need to confess my failure to God and to those I've offended and then change my mind about the sin. I just can't keep on sinning, taking my sin's impact lightly.

Second, the Scriptures teach that *we've got to forgive*. Forgiveness is not optional equipment in the Christian life. We are commanded to forgive because we've been forgiven.

To forgive others means we give up the right to punish them. We no longer hold the offenses against them.

Forgiveness is at the heart of Christianity. Your marriage—and mine—must be the union of two people who are not willing to allow anything to come between them.

Discuss: Are you usually quick to ask forgiveness— and to extend it? Why is it often hard to be quick to forgive those who fail us? Are you still punishing your spouse for something hurtful he or she said or did?

Pray: Thank God for His willingness to forgive you, and pray for a heart willing to forgive those who fail you.

FORGIVENESS IS NOT OPTIONAL EQUIPMENT IN THE CHRISTIAN LIFE.

LEAVE IT TO HEAVEN

Never take your own revenge, beloved,
but leave room for the wrath of God, for it is written,
"Vengeance is Mine, I will repay," says the Lord.

ROMANS 12:19

This classified ad actually appeared in a San Francisco area newspaper:

> For sale: 1984 Mercedes, 240 SL. Loaded. First $50 takes it. 868-5737.

Not believing his eyes, a man called the number to see if the "$50" was a misprint. A woman assured him it wasn't, so the man rushed to her home and gave her $50 in cash. As she handed him the title to the luxurious automobile, he asked the obvious question: "Why are you selling a Mercedes for $50?"

"Well," she explained, "my husband just phoned me from Las Vegas. He's there with his secretary, and he said he's leaving me. He went broke gambling, and he asked me to sell the Mercedes and send him half of what I get for it."

This woman got what she thought was sweet revenge. Unfortunately, it's a pattern of behavior that often creeps into families that aren't breaking up as well as those struck by the tragedy of divorce. We justify getting back at people when they take advantage of us. We think accounts need to be evened up.

Why does the Bible challenge such thinking and behavior? Why are we to leave vengeance to God? Because He is the source of right and wrong—we are not. When your mate hurts you, it ultimately wounds God more than you. Furthermore, God is the One who can dispense forgiving grace to you when you hurt your mate.

To take on the right of getting back at others is basically a sign of pride. The apostle Paul's counsel "Bless those who persecute you" (Rom. 12:14) is followed closely by the command "Do not be proud" (v. 16, *NIV*). We dare not take for ourselves that which belongs to God.

Punishment belongs to Him. Marriages work better when we leave such lofty matters to heaven.

Discuss: What types of offenses typically lead you to seek revenge? How has your mate sought revenge against you?

Pray: Ask God to help you and your mate develop the humility to be more forgiving toward each other, leaving revenge in the hands of God.

WE JUSTIFY GETTING BACK
AT PEOPLE WHEN THEY
TAKE ADVANTAGE OF US.
WE THINK ACCOUNTS NEED
TO BE EVENED UP.

SATAN'S SCHEMES

In order that no advantage be taken of us by Satan;
for we are not ignorant of his schemes.

2 C O R I N T H I A N S 2 : 1 1

I've noticed that many Christians are somewhat naïve about the devices Satan uses to tempt us to follow him. The "harmless" office flirtation, the casual attitude toward immorality in the media—it's as though we were unaware that such schemes can wreck our homes.

The world isn't going to issue warnings. For instance, I've never seen the following warning on a movie at a video rental store:

> Caution: This movie contains provocative material that could create an addiction to pornography, cause infidelity and violence and result in the loss of your dignity and family.

If we are to stand the test, we will have to become more aware of Satan's tactics.

I find that there are certain times when I am more vulnerable to the enemy's schemes:

- *When I'm alone*—Like most people, I'm tempted when no one else is looking (e.g., when I'm away on a trip, isolated from those who know me).

- *When I'm with someone who's willing to be a part of Satan's scheme*—If the enemy can't get me when I am alone, he places me among people who tempt me to gossip or to go along with the crowd (to be a people pleaser).
- *When I'm tired*—When I am physically and emotionally tired, I become susceptible to erroneous thoughts about God, myself and others. I've learned that temptation is easier to withstand when I'm not living on the edge. I need to retreat periodically to allow God to replenish my strength.
- *When I think I can justify my actions*—I am constantly amazed at my ability to rationalize wrong choices.

We have a mistaken tendency to believe that these schemes and temptations decrease as we grow older. Biblically and practically speaking, my flesh is no better today than it was 40 years ago when I became a Christian. The mistake is made when we drop our guard to seemingly small temptations, giving the enemy an opportunity to get a foothold in our lives. "Be on the alert!" (1 Pet. 5:8).

Discuss: When are you most susceptible to the schemes of Satan? What schemes do you find him using in your own life?

Pray: Pray for one another that you will not drop your guard and be carried away by the deceitfulness of sin.

FAMOUS LAST WORDS

*It is better to go to a house of mourning than to
go to a house of feasting, because that is the end of every
man, and the living takes it to heart.*

ECCLESIASTES 7:2

While some people collect things like baseball cards, matchbooks and menus, I, I must confess, have a small and strange collection of my own: exit lines—the final utterances of the dying.

My collection of quotes is not as morbid as you may think. They not only tell you how a man died, but they also hint at how he lived. A person's last words are the bookend of the legacy he or she leaves.

Author Henry David Thoreau was known as an irreverent and arrogant individualist. Shortly before he died, his aunt asked him if he'd made his peace with God. Thoreau responded, "I didn't know we'd ever quarreled."

Contrast Thoreau's cynicism with the inspiring last words of the great evangelist D. L. Moody. He was reported to have turned to his sons by his bedside and said, "If God be your partner, make your plans large."

Some last lines are ominous whispers of a feared fate. Others shout the confident message, "This isn't it! Death is not the end." Ponder the contrast in these famous last words:

> Draw the curtain, the farce is played. —Francois Rabelais, sixteenth-century French philosopher and comic

> Our God is the God from whom cometh salvation. God is the Lord by whom we escape death. —Martin Luther

> I am abandoned by God and man . . . I shall go to hell. —Voltaire

> I enjoy heaven already in my soul. My prayers are all converted into praises. —Augustus Toplady, author of the great hymn "Rock of Ages"

> I am convinced that there is no hope. —Winston Churchill, whose vision and battle cry in life was "Never give up"

> I have pain . . . but I have peace, I have peace. —Richard Baxter, seventeenth-century Puritan theologian

What will your final words be? How do you want to be remembered? How is your life today an investment in the legacy you will leave?

Discuss: What would you like to have engraved on your tombstone? What would you like your last words to be?

Pray: Ask God to help your daily life be a living testimony to the way you hope to die.

A PERSON'S LAST WORDS TELL
YOU HOW A MAN DIED AND
HINT AT HOW HE LIVED.

THE FINAL WORDS OF OBADIAH HOLMES

So then, my beloved, just as you have always obeyed, . . .
work out your salvation with fear and trembling.

PHILIPPIANS 2:12

Obadiah Holmes was a godly man who, together with his wife, raised eight children in the 1600s and gave them a firm foundation in Christ. On December 16, 1675, knowing his end was near, Obadiah sat down to write a final letter to his children—little did he know that this amazing document would survive for another 10 generations. After addressing in this letter their firm foundation, he concluded with a list of challenging, practical ways to live out their faith:

> Be you content with your present condition and portion God has given you. Make a good use of what you have by making use of it for your comfort (solace). For meat, drink or apparel, it is the gift of God. Take care to live honestly, justly, quietly with love and peace among yourselves, your neighbors and, if possible, be at peace with all men.

In what you can, do good to all men, especially to such as fear the Lord. Forget not to entertain strangers, according to your ability; if it be done in sincerity, it will be accepted, especially if to a disciple in the name of a disciple. Do to all men as you would have them do to you.

If you would be Christ's disciples, you must know and consider that you must take up your cross and follow Him, through evil report and losses. But yet know, he that will lose his life for Him shall save it.

Thus, my dear children, have I according to my measure, as is my duty, counseled you. May the good Lord give you understanding in all things and by His Holy Spirit convince, reprove and instruct and lead you into all truth as it is in Jesus. So that when you have done your work here, He may receive you to glory. Now the God of truth and peace be with you, unto Whom I commit this and you, even to Him be glory forever and ever, Amen.

A powerful exhortation. Did it make a difference? Yes. Some 10 generations later, one of Obadiah's descendants is a man by the name of Dave Jones. Dave pastors a church in Georgia and, together with his wife, Peggy, is impacting thousands of marriages by speaking at FamilyLife Marriage Conferences.

Today, some 300 years later, Obadiah reminds us that nothing else we leave our children will ever be as important as a conviction that God must be everything to them.

Discuss: If you were to write a final letter to your children, what would you say?

Pray: Ask God to help you "number your days" (Ps. 90:12), live your life for Christ and raise your children according to His priorities.

S ince attending a FamilyLife Conference, the Millers have been too distracted to read their favorite books ...

another love story has their attention.

Get away for a romantic weekend together ...

WEEKEND TO REMEMBER

or join us for a life-changing, one-day conference!

I still Do

For more information or to receive a free brochure, call **1-800-FL-TODAY** (1-800-358-6329), 24 hours a day, or visit **www.familylife.com**

Familylife has been bringing couples the wonderful news of God's blueprints for marriage since 1976.

Today we are strengthening hundreds of thousands of homes each year in the United States and around the world through:

- ◆ **Weekend to Remember**™ conferences

- ◆ **I Still Do**® conferences

- ◆ **HomeBuilders Couples Series**® small-group Bible studies

- ◆ **"FamilyLife Today,"** our daily, half-hour radio program, and four other nationally syndicated broadcasts

- ◆ A comprehensive Web site, **www.familylife.com**, featuring marriage and parenting tips, daily devotions, conference information, and a wide range of resources for strengthening families

- ◆ Unique marriage and family **connecting resources**

Through these outreaches, FamilyLife is effectively developing godly families who reach the world one home at a time.

FAMILYLIFE™
Bringing Timeless Principles Home

Dennis Rainey, Executive Director
1-800-FL-TODAY (358-6329)
www.familylife.com

A division of Campus Crusade for Christ

Also from Dennis and Barbara Rainey

More Devotions for Drawing Near to God and One Another

Moments Together for Intimacy
Gift Hardcover • ISBN 08307.32489

Moments Together for Parents
Gift Hardcover • ISBN 08307.32497

Moments Together for
Growing Closer to God
Gift Hardcover • ISBN 08307.32500

Moments Together
for a Peaceful Home
Gift Hardcover • ISBN 08307.32519